Clever Lunchbox Puzzles

Fun Tear-Outs to Pack with Your Sandwiches

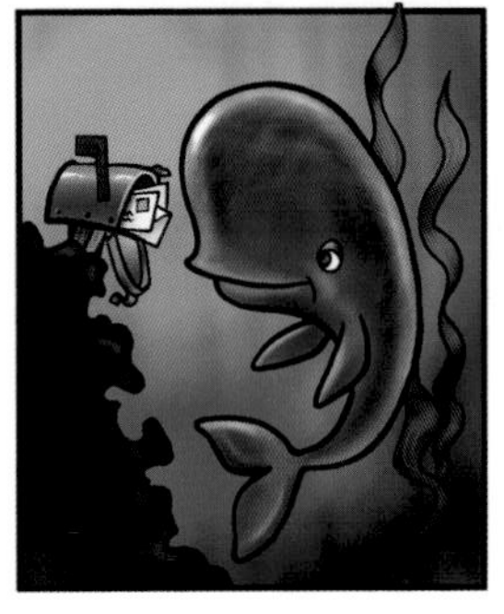

Steve Ryan

Illustrated by Jon Ottinger

Sterling Publishing Co., Inc.
New York

Edited by Jeanette Green
Designed by Chris DiStasio and Jeanette Green
Illustrated by Jon Ottinger

2 4 6 8 10 9 7 5 3 1

Published by Sterling Publishing Co., Inc.
387 Park Avenue South, New York, NY 10016

Distributed in Canada by Sterling Publishing
c/o Canadian Manda Group, 165 Dufferin Street
Toronto, Ontario, Canada M6K 3H6
Distributed in Great Britain and Europe by Chris Lloyd at Orca Book Services, Stanley House, Fleets Lane, Poole BH15 3AJ, England
Distributed in Australia by Capricorn Link (Australia) Pty. Ltd.
P.O. Box 704, Windsor, NSW 2756, Australia

Printed in China

Sterling ISBN 1-4027-1386-X

For information about custom editions, special sales, premium and corporate purchases, please contact Sterling Special Sales Department at 800-805-5489 or specialsales@sterlingpub.com.

The answer to the rebus on the title page is HOMEMADE COOKIES.
You'll find the other puzzles and answers inside the book.

CONTENTS

Introduction

Ready for a feast? Pack your lunchbox or sandwich bag each day with a fun tear-out sheet of one of these humorous and perplexing puzzles designed to stump, surprise, and entertain you. Then put on your thinking cap. Solve the puzzles yourself or share them with lunch buddies. On the back of each puzzle page you'll find a fun fact, a "Did You Know?" that's designed to raise eyebrows and reveal something fascinating.

We wanted to make each of these clever lunchbox picture puzzles visually delightful and enticing. We hope that they immediately capture your eye, flirt with your curiosity, and challenge your mind.

You won't need a pencil to enjoy these visual vexations. In this collection are rebuses, rhyming picture puzzles, fractured phrases, and scramblers, as well as puzzles that challenge you to find out what's wrong with the picture. Some puzzles are pushovers, others may require flexing mental muscles, and still others are really tough nuts to crack.

If you're up to the challenge, and we're sure you are, you're in for a terrific think test and a rib-tickling time with this daily dose of clever lunchbox puzzles. Later when you want to check your answers for the puzzle tear-outs, you'll find them in the remaining book margins. We've also listed them in the back of the book.

—Steve Ryan

About the Puzzles

SCRAMBLERS Each of these puzzles illustrates a two-word anagram puzzle. We give the scrambled letters and the illustration. All you have to do is unscramble two different words that describe the picture using the one given set of letters. For example, if we were to show the letters A C E E H R T and a picture of a classroom instructor taking a test with all the answers hidden up his sleeve, the answer would be CHEATER TEACHER (both contain the given identical scrambled letters).

FRACTURED PHRASES Each of these puzzles illustrates a well-known person, place, thing, or phrase illustrated with an unexpected rib-tickling twist. Your task is simply to reveal the phrase in the illustration. For example, if we were to show a person sitting on top of a huge ice cream sundae with a steering wheel and driving down a road, the answer would be SUNDAY DRIVER.

RHYME TIME I'm sure you've heard that "a picture is worth a thousand words." Well, that's not the case here. Each of these rhyming picture puzzles is worth only two words. That's because each puzzle illustrates a super-duper two-word rhyme-time experience that's silly to say and lots of fun to play. For example, if you were to see a puzzle showing Mickey Mouse's girlfriend after she went on a crash diet and lost a few too many pounds, the answer would be SKINNY MINNIE. Each two-word rhyming answer is just that easy—well, you be the judge.

WHAT'S WRONG WITH THIS PICTURE? Each of these puzzles has something blatantly wrong with it. We are always looking for the single thing that is most obviously wrong with the picture. Your task is to identify this one wrong element. For example, if we were to show an ice fisherman with a big fish that he had just proudly pulled through a tiny hole in the ice, the answer would be: It is impossible to catch such a big fish through such a tiny hole (or any variation of this answer).

REBUSES The rebuses in this book use easily recognized pictures combined with letters and words. If you can identify motion lines on the crack of a baseball bat as a "hit" or a sheep with lipstick and false eyelashes as a "ewe," you can solve these rebuses.

Here are a few tips to remember when solving a rebus. It's not necessary that the pictures relate to the phrase. The only requirement is that the pictures and symbols phonetically convey a pronunciation that's close to the phrase they represent. Plus signs are used to connect the pictures and letters to create one or more whole words. Flash marks or arrows often highlight a significant part of a picture. If a letter of the alphabet appears with quotation marks, say the letter. It's as easy A, B, C. If a letter or letters of the alphabet appear without quotation marks, then say them phonetically.

Scrambler

Use the given letters twice to unscramble two different words that describe the picture.

A B E R

Did You Know?

If very hot water is poured into a glass, the glass is more likely to break if the glass is thick rather than thin.

Hint for puzzle on page 7: The first word begins with B, and the second word begins with B.

Answer to puzzle on page 7: BARE BEAR

Fractured Phrase

Solve this puzzle by identifying the familiar phrase that's illustrated with an unusual twist.

Did You Know?

Honey is the only food that does not spoil the way most foods do.

Hint for puzzle on page 9: This is one way for commuters to travel.

Answer to puzzle on page 9: CAR POOL

Rhyme Time

Solve this with a two-word rhyme like *snail jail* or *crazy daisy.*

Did You Know?

It is easier to shoot a hole-in-one in golf than it is to bowl a perfect 300 game in bowling.

Hint for puzzle on page 11: The initials are…B F.

Answer to puzzle on page 11: BEAVER FEVER

What's Wrong with This Picture?

Identify the single most obvious thing wrong with this picture.

Did You Know?

The penny was the first U.S. coin to have the portrait of a president on it. Lincoln still appears on the coin.

Hint for puzzle on page 13: Focus on the flags.

Answer to puzzle on page 13: The wind cannot blow the two flags in opposite directions.

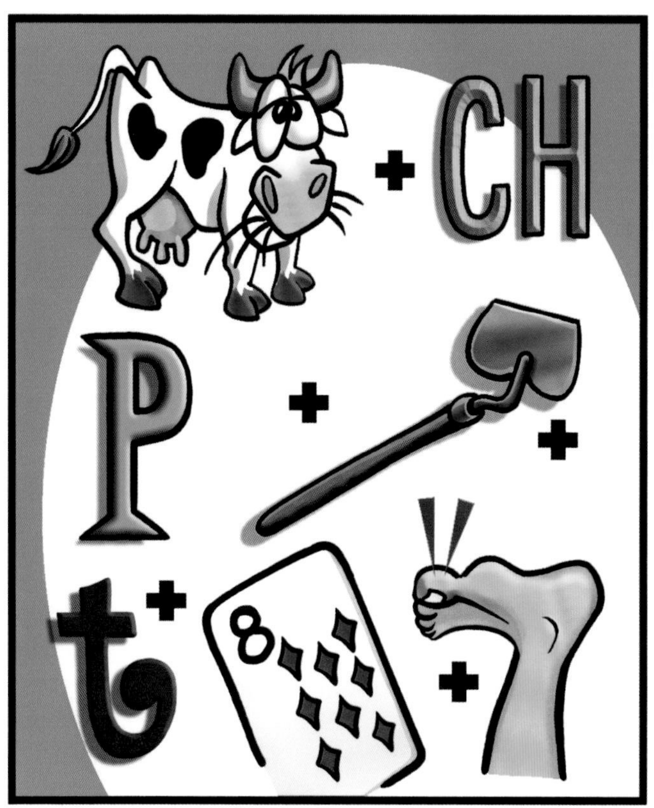

REBUS

Solve this familiar phrase by phonetically sounding out the pictures, letters, and words.

Did You Know?

The lobster can lose an entire leg and later completely grow a new one.

Hint for puzzle on page 15: This is a 2-word phrase. The initials are...C P.

Answer to puzzle on page 15: COUCH POTATO

Scrambler

Use the given letters twice to unscramble two different words that describe the picture.

O S B S

Did You Know?

Greenland contains more ice than greenery. The Vikings named it Greenland to lure potential colonists.

Hint for puzzle on page 17: The first word begins with B, and the second word begins with S.

Answer to puzzle on page 17: BOSS SOBS.

Fractured Phrase

Solve this puzzle by identifying the familiar phrase that's illustrated with an unusual twist.

Did You Know?

High white chef's hats traditionally have 100 pleats. These 100 pleats symbolize the 100 different ways to cook an egg.

Hint for puzzle on page 19: This is an activity for cowboys.

Answer to puzzle on page 19: CATTLE DRIVE

Rhyme Time

Solve this with a two-word rhyme like *snail jail* or *crazy daisy.*

Did You Know?

More ants (population) live on this planet than any other kind of insect.

Hint for puzzle on page 21: The initials are...B P.

Answer to puzzle on page 21: BIG PIG

What's Wrong with This Picture?

Identify the single most obvious thing wrong with this picture.

Did You Know?

There are more cows in the country of India than in any other country in the world. Approximately 250 million...

Hint for puzzle on page 23: Focus on the four points of the compass.

Answer to puzzle on page 23: South and East are in the wrong position.

REBUS

Solve this familiar phrase by phonetically sounding out the pictures, letters, and words.

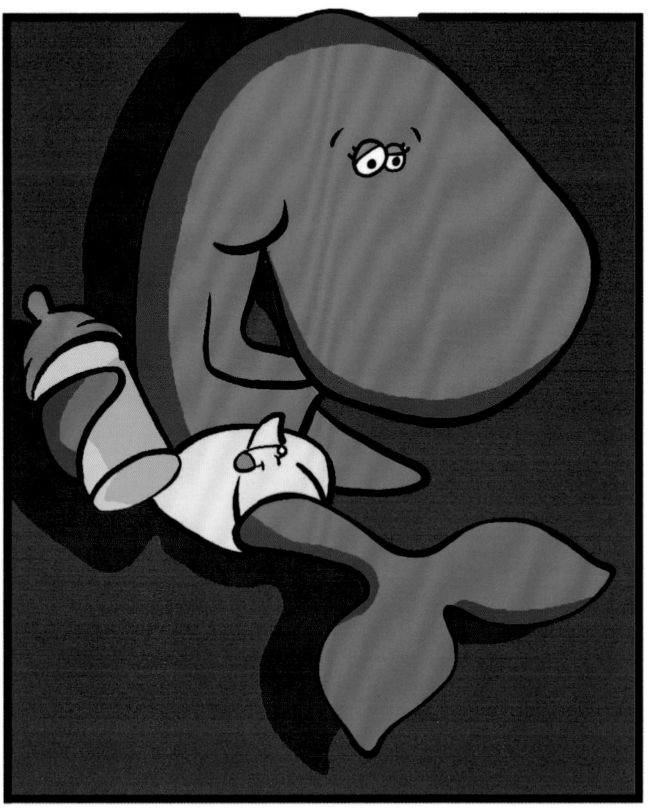

Did You Know?

A baby blue whale's growth rate is so fast that it can put on as much as 10 pounds (4.5 kg) an hour. During the first seven or eight months, it can gain about 33,000 pounds (14,850 kg).

Hint for puzzle on page 25: This is a 2-word phrase. The initials are...D T.

Answer to puzzle on page 25: DOUBLE TROUBLE

SCRAMBLER

Use the given letters twice to unscramble two different words that describe the picture.

A C L M

Did You Know?

A camel's hump is nearly all fat and can weigh up to 80 pounds.

Hint for puzzle on page 27: The first word begins with C, and the second word begins with C.

Answer to puzzle on page 27: CALM CLAM

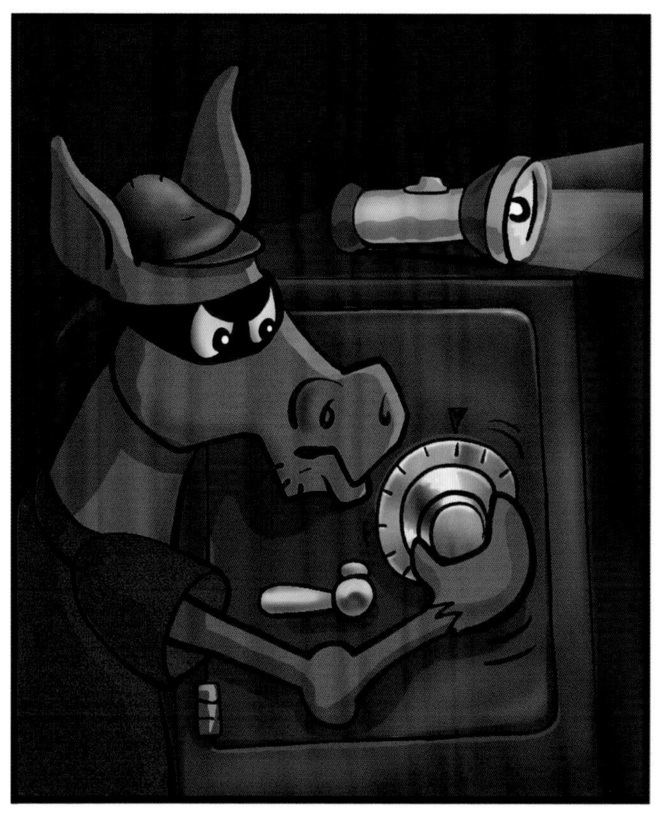

Fractured Phrase

Solve this puzzle by identifying the familiar phrase that's illustrated with an unusual twist.

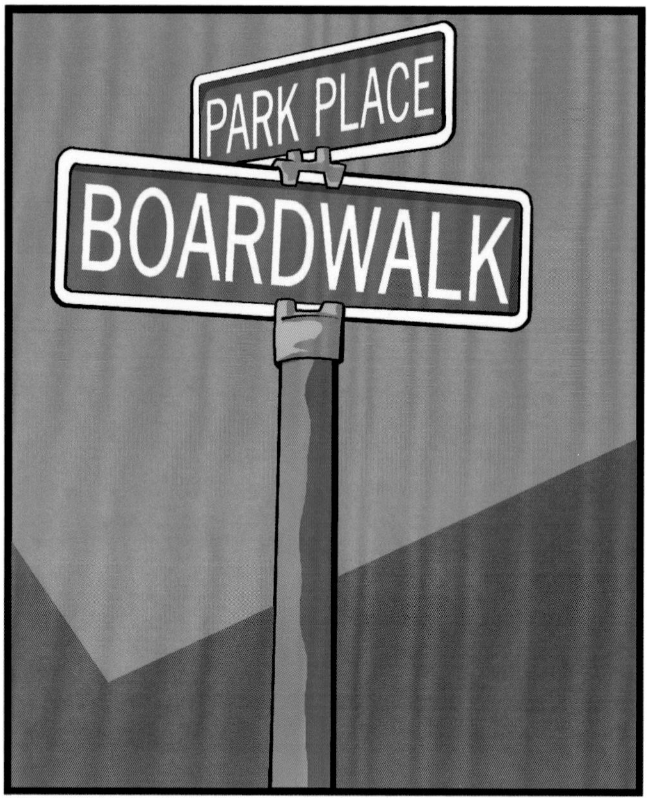

Did You Know?

The board in the game of Monopoly is based on actual street names found in Atlantic City, New Jersey.

Hint for puzzle on page 29: This was punishable by hanging in the Old West.

Answer to puzzle on page 29: HORSE THIEF

Rhyme Time

Solve this with a two-word rhyme like *snail jail* or *crazy daisy.*

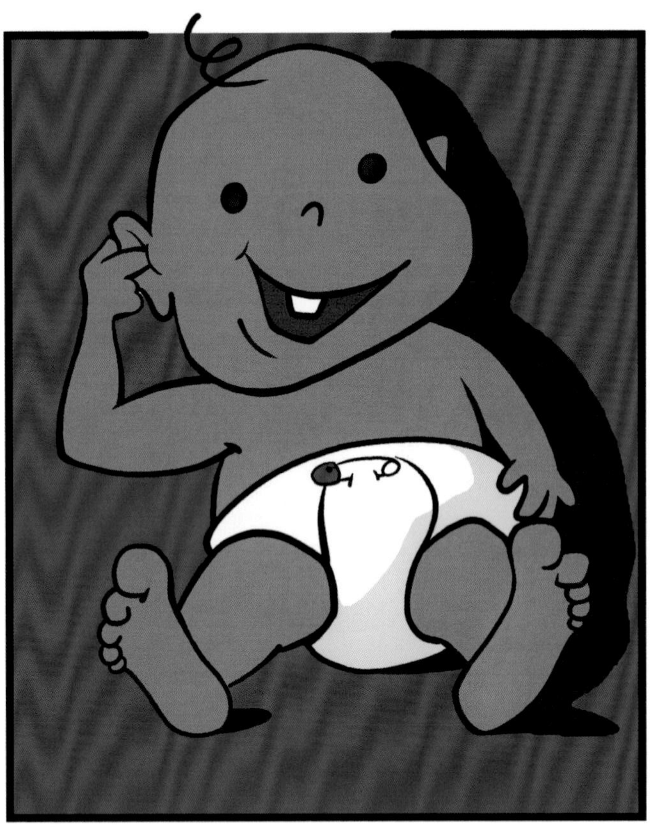

Did You Know?

The anvil, the hammer, and the stirrup bones of the ear are the only bones in the body that are fully developed at birth and never grow any larger.

Hint for puzzle on page 31: The initials are...B P.

Answer to puzzle on page 31: BONY PONY

What's Wrong with This Picture?

Identify the single most obvious thing wrong with this picture.

Did You Know?

M & M's were originally created for the U.S. military so that soldiers could carry a chocolate candy in their pockets that wouldn't melt.

Hint for puzzle on page 33: Focus on the crescent moon.

Answer to puzzle on page 33: We cannot view stars through the dark side of the moon.

REBUS

Solve this familiar phrase by phonetically sounding out the pictures, letters, and words.

Did You Know?

There is a breed of dog called basenji that cannot bark like other dogs. Its sound most closely resembles yodeling.

Hint for puzzle on page 35: This is a 4-word phrase. The initials are...X M T S.

Answer to puzzle on page 35: X MARKS THE SPOT.

SCRAMBLER

Use the given letters twice to unscramble two different words that describe the picture.

E E N P R S T

Did You Know?

In the country of Iceland the telephone book is not alphabetized according to last names. It is alphabetized according to first names.

Hint for puzzle on page 37: The first word begins with S, and the second word begins with P.

Answer to puzzle on page 37: SERPENT PRESENT

Fractured Phrase

Solve this puzzle by identifying the familiar phrase that's illustrated with an unusual twist.

Did You Know?

The fastest swimming creature in any body of water is the sailfish. Its top speed is 68 miles per hour (almost 109 kilometers per hour).

Hint for puzzle on page 39: This is a product for a house-trained cat.

Answer to puzzle on page 39: KITTY LITTER

Rhyme Time

Solve this with a two-word rhyme like *snail jail* or *crazy daisy.*

Did You Know?

The Great Wall of China took almost 2,000 years to build.

Hint for puzzle on page 41: The initials are...C C.

Answer to puzzle on page 41: CHARRED CARD

What's Wrong with This Picture?

Identify the single most obvious thing wrong with this picture.

Did You Know?

The opposite sides of a standard die always add up to seven.

Hint for puzzle on page 43: Focus on the doorknob.

Answer to puzzle on page 43: The doorknob and hinges are on the same side of the door.

REBUS

Solve this familiar phrase by phonetically sounding out the pictures, letters, and words.

Did You Know?

If an octopus gets a cut or a scrape and bleeds, its blood will come out blue.

Hint for puzzle on page 45: This is a 5-word phrase. The initials are...L I O L I.

Answer to puzzle on page 45: LIKE IT OR LUMP IT.

SCRAMBLER

Use the given letters twice to unscramble two different words that describe the picture.

E H O R S

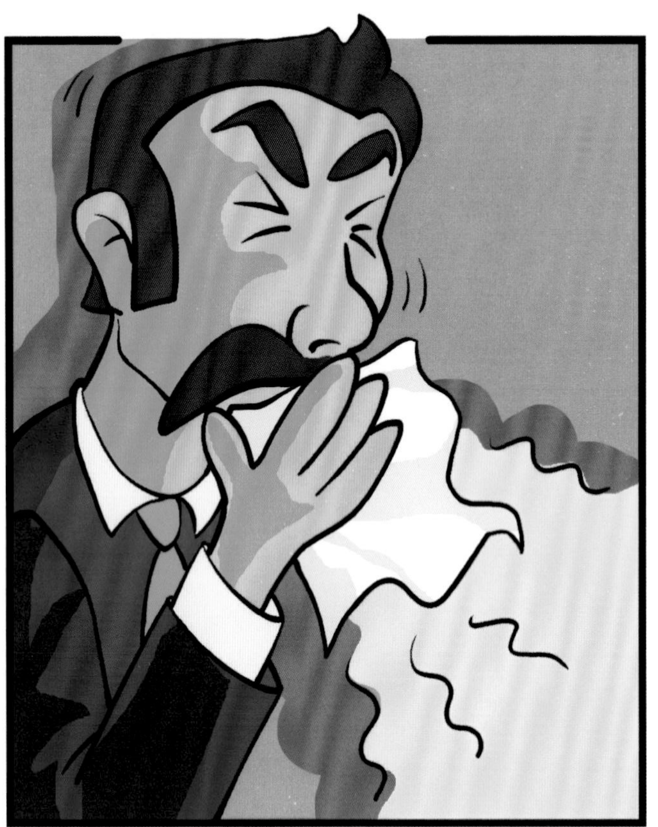

Did You Know?

It's impossible to sneeze and keep one's eyes open at the same time.

Hint for puzzle on page 47: The first word begins with S, and the second word begins with H.

Answer to puzzle on page 47: SHORE HORSE

Did You Know?

If you lived on the Equator, the hottest months of the year would be March and September.

Hint for puzzle on page 49: Class is held here in the evening.

Answer to puzzle on page 49: (K)NIGHT SCHOOL

Fractured Phrase

Solve this puzzle by identifying the fam i li
phrase that's illustrated with an unusual tv

Rhyme Time

Solve this with a two-word rhyme like *snail jail* or *crazy daisy.*

Did You Know?

Thomas Jefferson was inspired to invent the swivel chair because he didn't like his stationary desk chair.

Hint for puzzle on page 51: The initials are...F C.

Answer to puzzle on page 51: FLAT CAT

What's Wrong with This Picture?

Identify the single most obvious thing wrong with this picture.

Did You Know?

Lightning always travels at exactly the speed of light.

Hint for puzzle on page 53: Focus on the knees of the flamingo.

Answer to puzzle on page 53: The knees of the flamingo bend backward, not forward like human knees.

Rebus

Solve this familiar phrase by phonetically sounding out the pictures, letters, and words.

Did You Know?

You can get a green banana to ripen faster by putting it in a paper bag.

Hint for puzzle on page 55: This is a 2-word phrase. The initials are...M O.

Answer to puzzle on page 55: MICROWAVE OVEN

SCRAMBLER

Use the given letters twice to unscramble two different words that describe the picture.

A C E P S

Did You Know?

Because of extreme weather conditions, there are no railroads in Iceland.

Hint for puzzle on page 57: The first word begins with S, and the second word begins with C.

Answer to puzzle on page 57: SPACE CAPES

Fractured Phrase

Solve this puzzle by identifying the familiar phrase that's illustrated with an unusual twist.

Did You Know?

The first person to go over Niagara Falls in a barrel was a woman. Anna Edson Taylor did it in 1901.

Hint for puzzle on page 59: This is someone who tells your fortune.

Answer to puzzle on page 59: PALM READER

Rhyme Time

Solve this with a two-word rhyme like *snail jail* or *crazy daisy.*

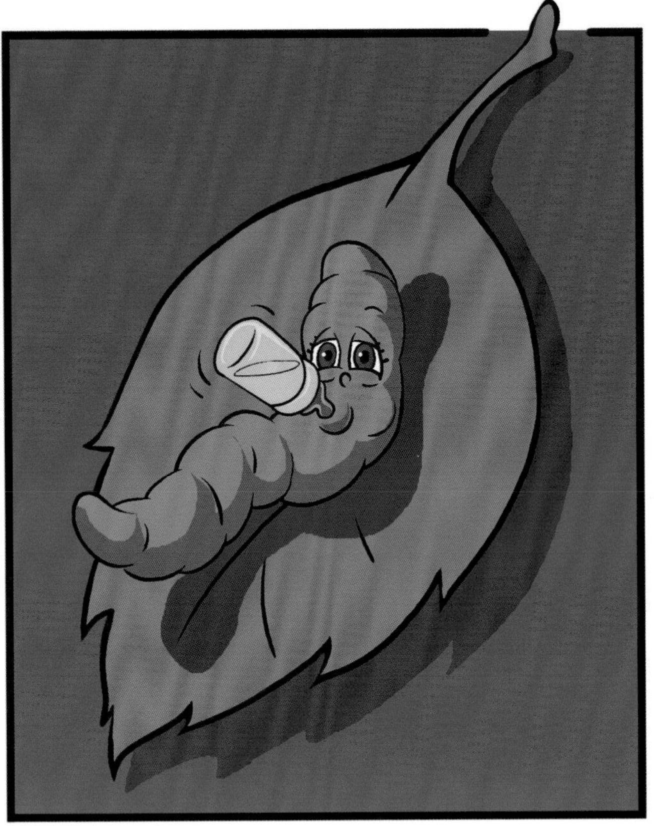

Did You Know?

When glowworms mature, they turn into fireflies (what some people call lightning bugs).

Hint for puzzle on page 61: The initials are...H B.

Answer to puzzle on page 61: HAIRY BERRY

What's Wrong with This Picture?

Identify the single most obvious thing wrong with this picture.

Did You Know?

The only mosquito bites you'll ever get will come from females. Males don't bite.

Hint for puzzle on page 63: Focus on what an ostrich cannot do.

Answer to puzzle on page 63: An ostrich cannot fly.

Rebus

Solve this familiar phrase by phonetically sounding out the pictures, letters, and words.

Did You Know?

More people live in Asia than any other continent. However, the continent with the most people per square mile (or square kilometer, for that matter) is Europe.

Hint for puzzle on page 65: This is a 4-word phrase. The initials are...N O Y B.

Answer to puzzle on page 65: NONE OF YOUR BEESWAX.

SCRAMBLER

Use the given letters twice to unscramble two different words that describe the picture.

A E P R S

Did You Know?

The most visible color you can paint your car is chartreuse (a bright yellow-green).

Hint for puzzle on page 67: The first word begins with S, and the second word begins with P.

Answer to puzzle on page 67: SPEAR PEARS

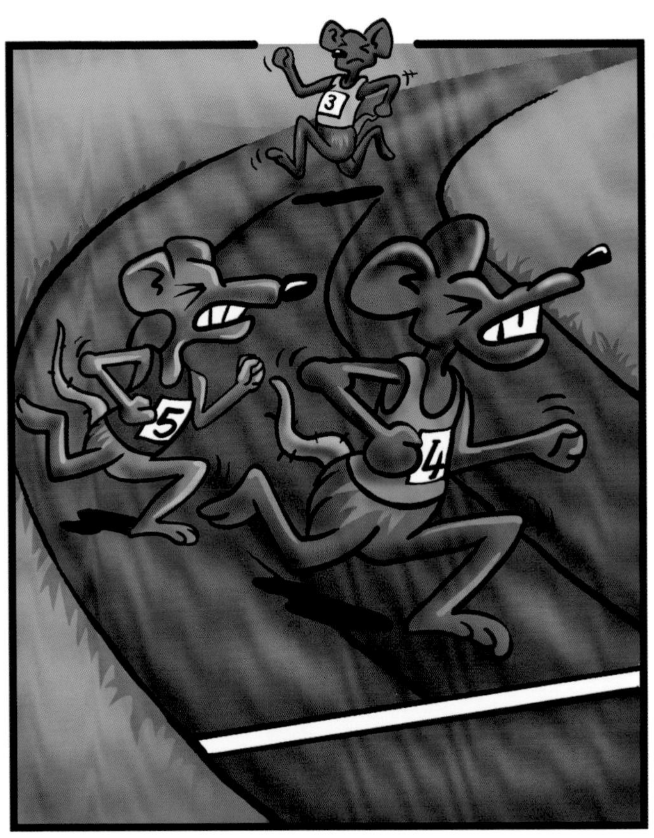

Fractured Phrase

Solve this puzzle by identifying the familiar phrase that's illustrated with an unusual twist.

Did You Know?

The parachute was actually invented more than 100 years before the invention of the airplane.

Hint for puzzle on page 69: This is the daily grind for many people.

Answer to puzzle on page 69: RAT RACE

RHYME TIME

Solve this with a two-word rhyme like *snail jail* or *crazy daisy.*

Did You Know?

The first time the words "In God We Trust" appeared on a U.S. coin was during the Civil War. It was a 2-cent piece.

Hint for puzzle on page 71: The initials are…P R.

Answer to puzzle on page 71: PRESIDENT'S RESIDENCE

What's Wrong with This Picture?

Identify the single most obvious thing wrong with this picture.

Did You Know?

At the Panama Canal, you can watch the sun rise over the Atlantic Ocean and set over the Pacific Ocean.

Hint for puzzle on page 73: Focus on the rainbow colors.

Answer to puzzle on page 73: The rainbow color spectrum is always red, orange, yellow, green, blue, then violet.

REBUS

Solve this familiar phrase by phonetically sounding out the pictures, letters, and words.

Did You Know?

The first U.S. President ever to be born in a hospital was Jimmy Carter.

Hint for puzzle on page 75: This is a 5-word phrase. The initials are...P O Y T C.

Answer to puzzle on page 75: PUT ON YOUR THINKING CAP.

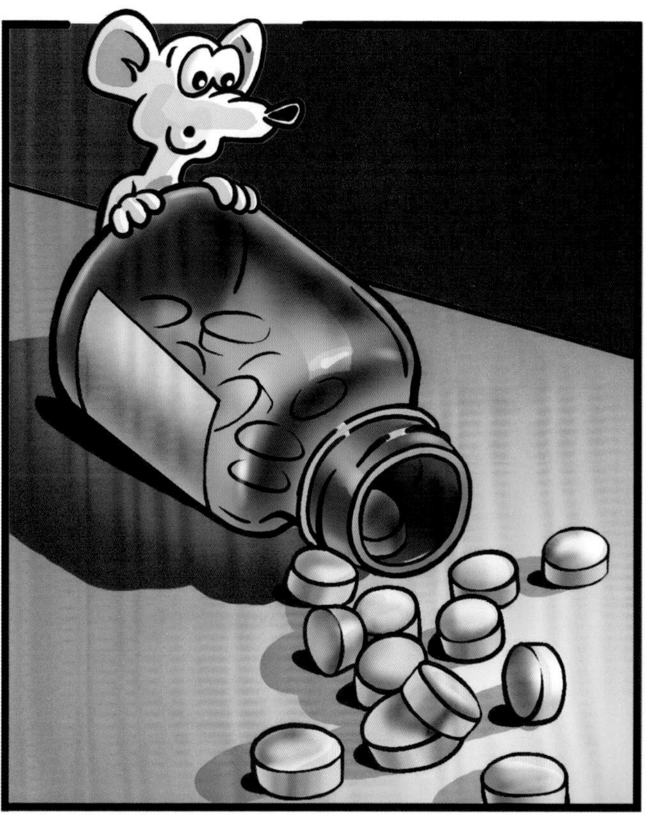

SCRAMBLER

Use the given letters twice to unscramble two different words that describe the picture.

P L I S L

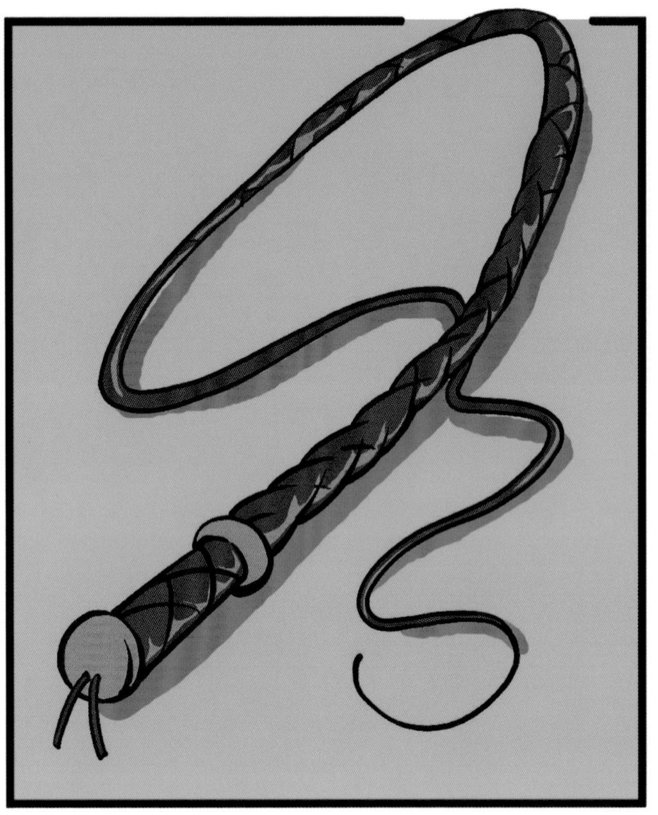

Did You Know?

A whip makes a cracking noise because its tip moves faster than the speed of sound.

Hint for puzzle on page 77: The first word begins with S, and the second word begins with P.

Answer to puzzle on page 77: SPILL PILLS

Fractured Phrase

Solve this puzzle by identifying the familiar phrase that's illustrated with an unusual twist.

Did You Know?

Genuine ivory only comes from three sources: the tusks of elephants, boars, and walruses.

Hint for puzzle on page 79: This is something that happens in the night sky.

Answer to puzzle on page 79: SHOOTING STAR

Rhyme Time

Solve this with a two-word rhyme like *snail jail* or *crazy daisy.*

Did You Know?

Contrary to popular belief, not every snowflake has six sides (hexagonal shape). There are many types of snow crystals. Some have twelve arms, for instance.

Hint for puzzle on page 81: The initials are...S B.

Answer to puzzle on page 81: SOCCER BLOCKER

What's Wrong with This Picture?

Identify the single most obvious thing wrong with this picture.

Did You Know?

The largest (stepped) pyramid in the world is not found in Egypt. It's located in Mexico.

Hint for puzzle on page 83: Focus on the legs.

Answer to puzzle on page 83: Spiders have eight legs.

REBUS

Solve this familiar phrase by phonetically sounding out the pictures, letters, and words.

Did You Know?

The average meteorite is actually only the size of a grain of sand, weighing 0.0005 ounce (0.014 grams).

Hint for puzzle on page 85: This is a 4-word phrase. The initials are...S R A R.

Answer to puzzle on page 85: SHAKE, RATTLE, AND ROLL.

SCRAMBLER

Use the given letters twice to unscramble two different words that describe the picture.

A B E L S T

Did You Know?

The music to what we know today as "Twinkle, Twinkle, Little Star" was written by Mozart. Jane Taylor wrote the lyrics in 1806.

Hint for puzzle on page 87: The first word begins with S, and the second word begins with T.

Answer to puzzle on page 87: STABLE TABLES

Fractured Phrase

Solve this puzzle by identifying the familiar phrase that's illustrated with an unusual twist.

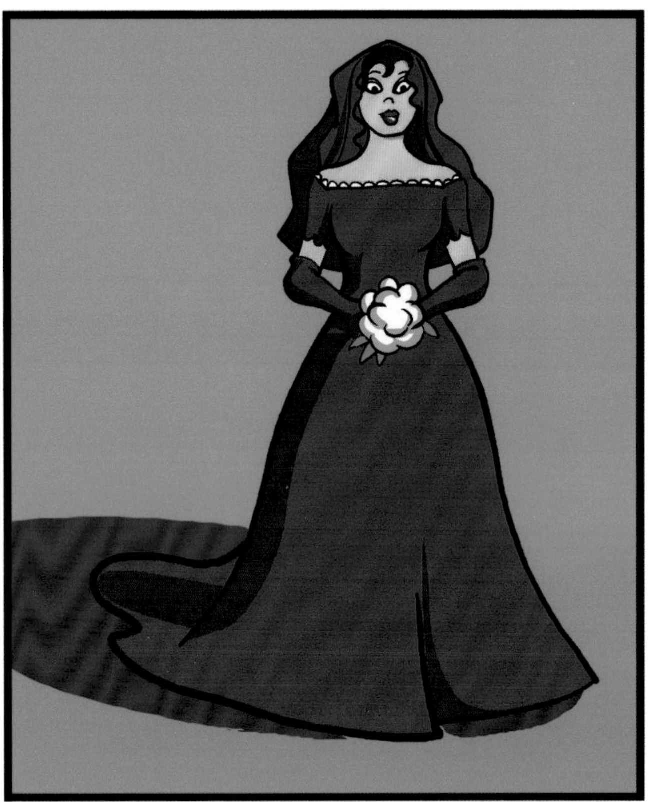

Did You Know?

In China, the usual color of a bride's wedding gown is red.

Hint for puzzle on page 89: This is an academic contest.

Answer to puzzle on page 89: SPELLING BEE

Rhyme Time

Solve this with a two-word rhyme like *snail jail* or *crazy daisy.*

Did You Know?

On the Wright Brothers' first successful flight, they only flew a distance of 120 feet (that's 36 meters).

Hint for puzzle on page 91: The initials are...S D or W P.

Answer to puzzle on page 91: SOGGY DOGGY or WET PET

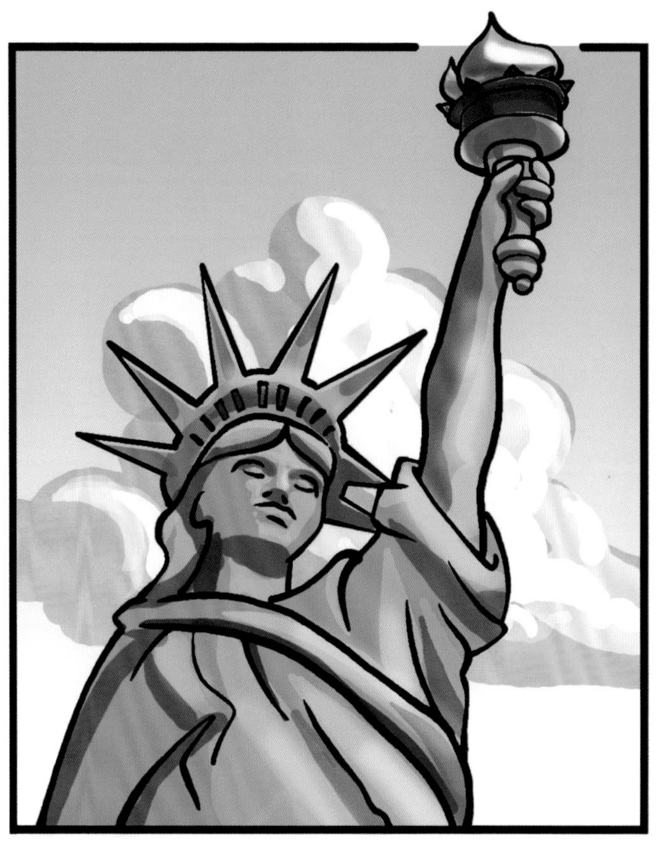

What's Wrong with This Picture?

Identify the single most obvious thing wrong with this picture.

Did You Know?

When Dalmatian puppies are born, they have no spots. They're born pure white. The spots begin to appear three to four weeks later.

Hint for puzzle on page 93: Focus on the torch.

Answer to puzzle on page 93: Miss Liberty is holding her torch in the wrong hand.

Rebus

Solve this familiar phrase by phonetically sounding out the pictures, letters, and words.

Did You Know?

Daylight saving time made its debut in the United States in the spring of 1918. In England, daylight saving time is called summer time.

Hint for puzzle on page 95: This is a 3-word phrase. The initials are...S Y C.

Answer to puzzle on page 95: STOP YOUR COMPLAINING.

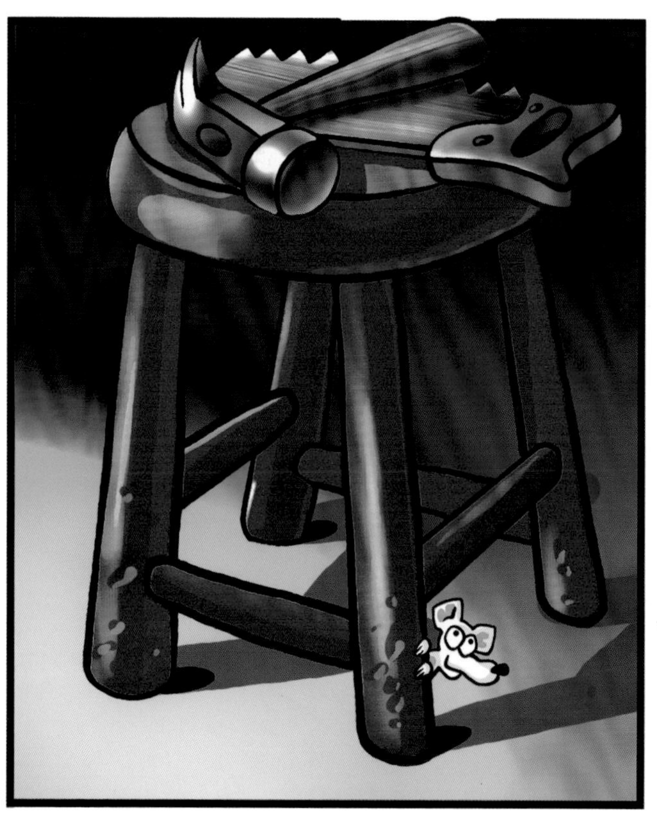

SCRAMBLER

Use the given letters twice to unscramble two different words that describe the picture.

L O O S T

Did You Know?

During his lifetime artist Vincent Van Gogh sold only one painting. Today his paintings rank among the most valuable artworks ever painted.

Hint for puzzle on page 97: The first word begins with S, and the second word begins with T.

Answer to puzzle on page 97: STOOL TOOLS

Fractured Phrase

Solve this puzzle by identifying the familiar phrase that's illustrated with an unusual twist.

Did You Know?

Flamingos turn pink because of the food they eat, particularly shrimp.

Hint for puzzle on page 99: These large flowers produce edible seeds.

Answer to puzzle on page 99: SUNFLOWERS

Rhyme Time

Solve this with a two-word rhyme like *snail jail* or *crazy daisy.*

Answer to puzzle on page 101: STAR CAR

Did You Know?

The Emperor moth has sensory hairs on its antennae that can detect a moth of the opposite sex from 3 miles (5 kilometers) away.

Hint for puzzle on page 101: The initials are...S C.

What's Wrong with This Picture?

Identify the single most obvious thing wrong with this picture.

Answer to puzzle on page 103: Chickens cannot swim.

Did You Know?

A 10-gallon (38 liter) hat can only hold about 2 quarts (1.9 liters) of liquid.

Hint for puzzle on page 103: Focus on what chickens can't do.

Rebus

Solve this familiar phrase by phonetically sounding out the pictures, letters, and words.

Did You Know?

The garter snake does not lay eggs. It bears live young, just as mammals do.

Hint for puzzle on page 105: This is a 4-word phrase. The initials are...T S N S.

Answer to puzzle on page 105: THOU SHALL NOT STEAL.

SCRAMBLER

Use the given letters twice to unscramble two different words that describe the picture.

N A T

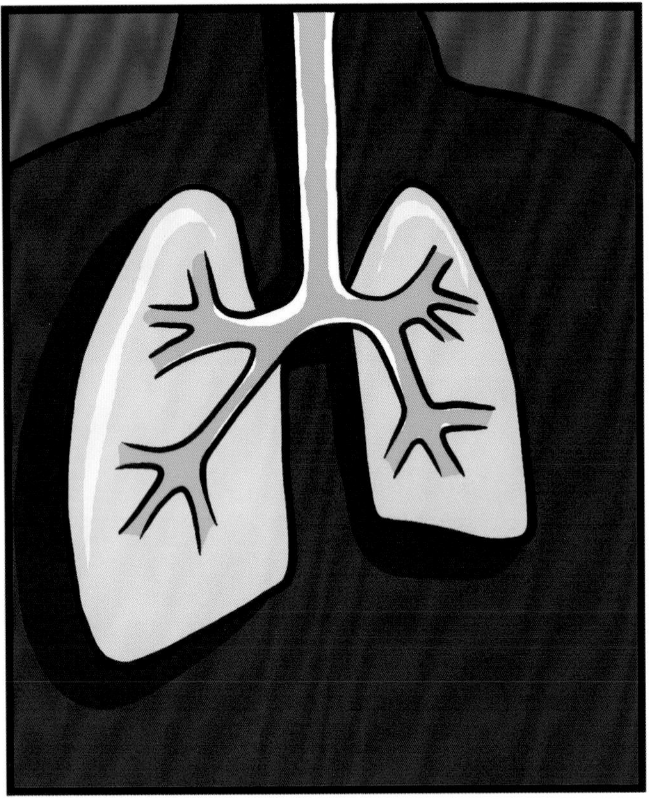

Did You Know?

In the human body, the right lung is larger than the left lung. Only in extremely rare cases where the heart is on the opposite side of the chest would the left lung be larger.

Hint for puzzle on page 107: The first word begins with T, and the second word begins with A.

Answer to puzzle on page 107: TAN ANT

Fractured Phrase

Solve this puzzle by identifying the familiar phrase that's illustrated with an unusual twist.

Did You Know?

The South Pole is colder than the North Pole. Better pack an extra pair of long johns!

Hint for puzzle on page 109: The outlaw Jesse James was one of these.

Answer to puzzle on page 109: TRAIN ROBBER

Rhyme Time

Solve this with a two-word rhyme like *snail jail* or *crazy daisy.*

Did You Know?

The highest waterfall in the United States is Yosemite Falls found on Yosemite Creek in California. It was carved by a prehistoric glacier.

Hint for puzzle on page 111: The initials are...W M.

Answer to puzzle on page 111: WHALE MAIL

What's Wrong with This Picture?

Identify the single most obvious thing wrong with this picture.

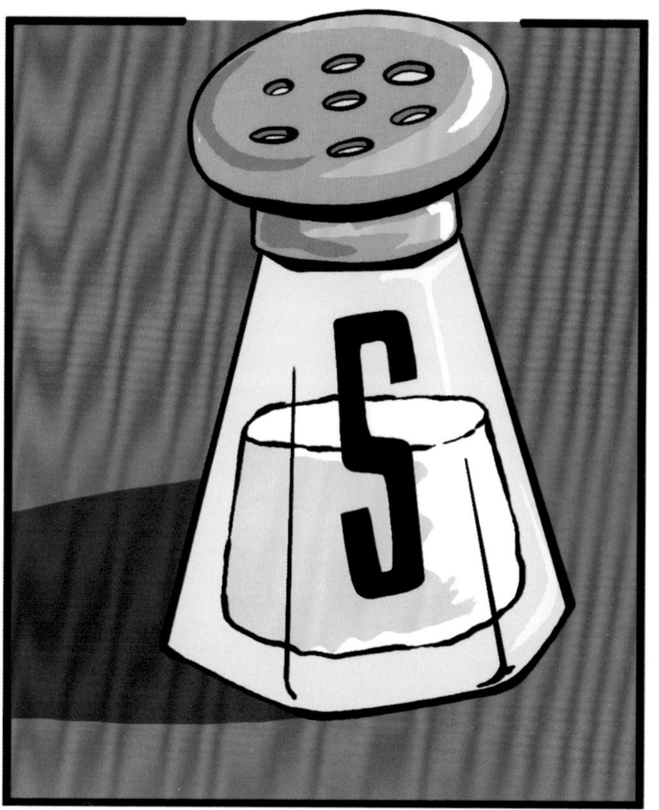

Did You Know?

The saltiest body of water in the world is the Dead Sea.

Hint for puzzle on page 113: Focus on the tennis ball.

Answer to puzzle on page 113: A tennis ball will not sink in water.

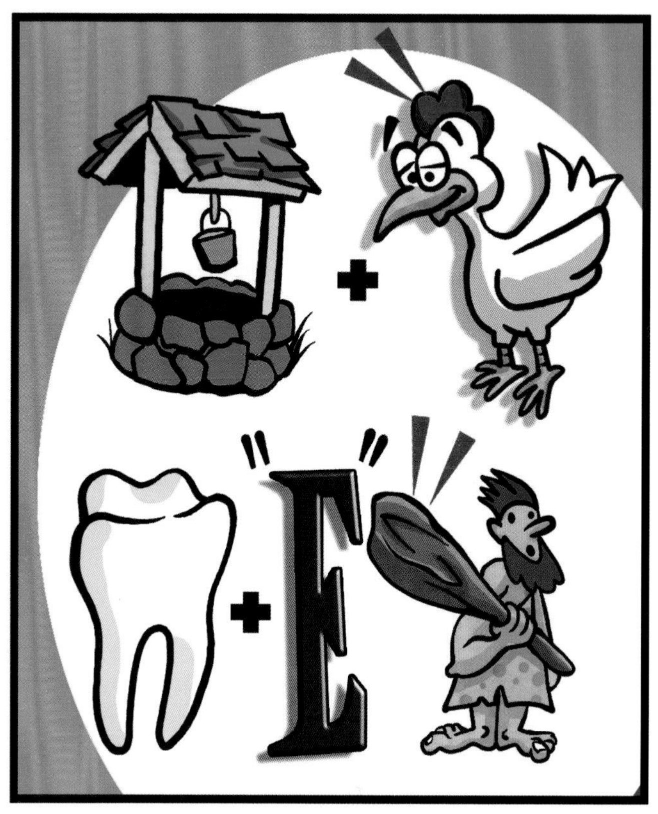

Rebus

Solve this familiar phrase by phonetically sounding out the pictures, letters, and words.

Did You Know?

Delaware was the first of the original thirteen colonies to be admitted to the Union.

Hint for puzzle on page 115: This is a 4-word phrase. The initials are...W T T C.

Answer to puzzle on page 115: WELCOME TO THE CLUB.

SCRAMBLER

Use the given letters twice to unscramble two different words that describe the picture.

O B R E D M O

Did You Know?

The fastest cat (feline) can run faster than the fastest dog. The cheetah has been clocked at 70 mph (112 kph) and the greyhound at just under 40 mph (64 kph).

Hint for puzzle on page 117: The first word begins with B, and the second word begins with B.

Answer to puzzle on page 117: BEDROOM BOREDOM

Fractured Phrase

Solve this puzzle by identifying the familiar phrase that's illustrated with an unusual twist.

Did You Know?

The bark of redwood trees is fairly fire-resistant. Fires do, however, burn the leaves and may begin "inside" the trees after, say, being struck by lightning.

Hint for puzzle on page 119: This animal is trained to guard your home.

Answer to puzzle on page 119: WATCH DOG

Rhyme Time

Solve this with a two-word rhyme like *snail jail* or *crazy daisy.*

Did You Know?

The most abundant domesticated bird in the world is the chicken.

Hint for puzzle on page 121: The initials are...W R.

Answer to puzzle on page 121: WITCHES' RICHES

What's Wrong with This Picture?

Identify the single most obvious thing wrong with this picture.

Did You Know?

The tails of most pigs curl in the same direction, clockwise.

Hint for puzzle on page 123: Focus on the colors of the lights.

Answer to puzzle on page 123: The red and green lights are in the wrong position.

Puzzle Answers

Answers are given by page numbers.

7, BARE BEAR

9, CAR POOL

11, BEAVER FEVER

13, The wind cannot blow two flags in opposite directions.

15, COUCH POTATO

17, BOSS SOBS.

19, CATTLE DRIVE

21, BIG PIG

23, South and East are in the wrong position.

25, DOUBLE TROUBLE

27, CALM CLAM

29, HORSE THIEF

31, BONY PONY

33, We cannot view stars through the dark side of the moon.

35, X MARKS THE SPOT.

37, SERPENT PRESENT

39, KITTY LITTER

41, CHARRED CARD

43, The doorknob and hinges are on the same side of the door.

45, LIKE IT OR LUMP IT.

47, SHORE HORSE

49, (K)NIGHT SCHOOL

51, FLAT CAT

53, The knees of the flamingo bend backward, not forward like human knees.

55, MICROWAVE OVEN

57, SPACE CAPES

59, PALM READER

61, HAIRY BERRY
63, An ostrich cannot fly.
65, NONE OF YOUR BEESWAX.
67, SPEAR PEARS
69, RAT RACE
71, PRESIDENT'S RESIDENCE
73, The rainbow color spectrum is always red, orange, yellow, green, blue, then violet.
75, PUT ON YOUR THINKING CAP.
77, SPILL PILLS
79, SHOOTING STAR
81, SOCCER BLOCKER
83, Spiders have eight legs.
85, SHAKE, RATTLE, AND ROLL.
87, STABLE TABLES
89, SPELLING BEE
91, SOGGY DOGGY or WET PET
93, Miss Liberty is holding her torch in the wrong hand.
95, STOP YOUR COMPLAINING.
97, STOOL TOOLS
99, SUNFLOWERS
101, STAR CAR
103, Chickens cannot swim.
105, THOU SHALL NOT STEAL.
107, TAN ANT
109, TRAIN ROBBER
111, WHALE MAIL
113, A tennis ball will not sink in water.
115, WELCOME TO THE CLUB.
117, BEDROOM BOREDOM
119, WATCH DOG
121, WITCHES' RICHES
123, The red and green lights are in the wrong position.

About the Author

Puzzle master Steve Ryan has created over 12,000 brain-busting bafflers. As a virtuoso of vexation, he has been inventing games and puzzles since childhood. His Puzzles & Posers and Zig-Zag newspaper features have appeared through Copley News Service in newspapers across the United States for over 25 years.

Mr. Ryan co-created and developed the television game show *Blockbusters* for game-show packager Mark Goodson. He has written for television's *Password Plus, Trivia Trap, Body Language,* and *Catch Phrase.* He also created the pricing game Now & Then for *The Price Is Right* and created all rebus puzzles for the television show *Classic Concentration.* His one-of-a-kind rebus creations are also utilized in Bally Gaming's Concentration slot machine.

Mr. Ryan has created many lottery games for such television shows as "The Big Spin" in California, "Bonus Bonanza" in Massachusetts, "Flamingo Fortune" in Florida, "Instant Riches" in Illinois, "Second Chance Sweepstakes" in Ohio, "Super Cash Sweepstakes" in Iowa, "New York Wired," and "Power Ball" the multi-state lottery. A few of his games featured in lottery game shows include Capsize, Force Field, Gold Rush, High Roller, Splashdown, Vortex, Wrecking Ball, and Zero Gravity. His lottery games have appeared on the television shows *A Chance de Ouro* in Brazil, *Telemazli* in Hungary, *Bingo-Lotto* in Lithuania, *Telelotto* in Estonia, and *Win 'n Spin* and *Zama Zama* in South Africa.

Mr. Ryan has written many puzzle books for Sterling Publishing Co., Inc., including *Sit & Solve Pencil Puzzles, Lunchbox Puzzles, Mystifying Math Puzzles, Pencil Puzzles, Challenging Pencil Puzzlers, Test Your Puzzle IQ, Test Your Word Play IQ, Test Your Math IQ, Rhyming Picture Puzzles, Great Rebus Puzzles*, and *Classic Concentration.*

He co-authored with David Schwartz and Fred Wostbrock *The Encyclopedia of TV Game Shows,* the most comprehensive book of its kind. Most recently, Mr. Ryan and Mr. Wostbrock have co-authored *The Ultimate TV Game Show Book.*

His puzzles have appeared in the magazines *Games, Nickelodeon, World of Puzzles, Games & Puzzles,* and numerous other periodicals. His puzzle books are distributed worldwide, and some have been translated into Spanish, French, Portuguese, Dutch, Russian, and Czech.

For more fun and games, log on to:

www.SteveRyanGames.com